Easy and Fun
Free-Motion Quilting

Easy and Fun
Free-Motion Quilting

Frames, Fillers, Hundreds of Ideas

Eva A. Larkin

Martingale®
Create with Confidence

Dedication

To God, who promises to never leave us and never forsake us, and to my dad, whose love constantly amazes me.

Easy and Fun Free-Motion Quilting:
Frames, Fillers, Hundreds of Ideas
© 2012 by Eva A. Larkin

Martingale®
19021 120th Ave. NE, Ste. 102
Bothell, WA 98011-9511 USA
ShopMartingale.com

Printed in China
17 16 15 14 13 12   8 7 6 5 4 3 2 1

Library of Congress Cataloging-in-Publication Data is available upon request.

ISBN: 978-1-60468-184-0

CREDITS

President & CEO: Tom Wierzbicki

Editor in Chief: Mary V. Green

Design Director: Paula Schlosser

Managing Editor: Karen Costello Soltys

Technical Editor: Laurie Baker

Copy Editor: Melissa Bryan

Production Manager: Regina Girard

Illustrator: Newgen and Connor Chin

Cover & Text Designer: Regina Girard

Photographer: Brent Kane

MISSION STATEMENT

Dedicated to providing quality products and service to inspire creativity.

Acknowledgments

I can't begin to thank my dad enough. His support and encouragement have been endless over the past couple of years. Like so many others, one day I found myself abandoned and bewildered after many years of marriage. I couldn't imagine any kind of future for myself and quite frankly didn't want one. But God, Dad, and Martingale gave me hope. God helped me hold on to the idea that I wasn't worthless and blessed my first book with Martingale. It seemed like every letter and call from Martingale came at just the right moment to give me the strength and courage to keep moving.

God also filled my heart with the dream of writing another free-motion quilting book, and my dad refused to let me give up on this dream, even on the days when I felt like I had only half a mind left. Every baby step I took to rebuild my life and work on "the book" was met with love and encouragement. Now I know that each day brings new hope, and dreams really do come true!

Contents

Introduction

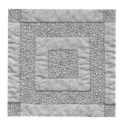 Hello Quilters,

Deciding how to quilt a completed quilt top has frustrated many quilters. It often seems like the only easy options available are stitching in the ditch, cross-hatching, or allover stippling. The other quilting possibilities are interesting, but they either have to be resized and traced or they were designed to be stitched on a long-arm quilting machine and are just too complicated for the everyday quilter.

Easy and Fun Free-Motion Quilting: Frames, Fillers, Hundreds of Ideas provides the everyday quilter with a fantastic variety of quilting designs created by combining stippling and short lines—and they can all be confidently stitched on a home sewing machine without hours of practice. The simple designs consist of two parts: base frames and fillers. The frames and fillers are made up of stippling and can be outlined with either straight or curved lines. The easy method of combining the base frames and fillers produces hundreds of exciting quilting designs that you can use on any size quilt block without resizing and tracing. Plus, each design comes with step-by-step instructions and detailed illustrations that clearly walk you through the process from start to finish.

I also have included a section on my free-motion quilting basics and an overview of my "wiggle" style of stippling. This will help those who feel uncomfortable with their stippling techniques to gain confidence and skill without hours of practice. You won't believe how easy it will be to get into the stippling groove and achieve and maintain consistent results, not only with the design but also with the thread tension and stitch length.

My hope for you is that this book will inspire you to finish those waiting quilt tops. I want you filled with excitement to select one of the beautiful designs and know you can stitch it with confidence. You'll discover that deciding how to "quilt as desired" can actually be a fun and rewarding process. So enjoy, and happy quilting!

—Eva

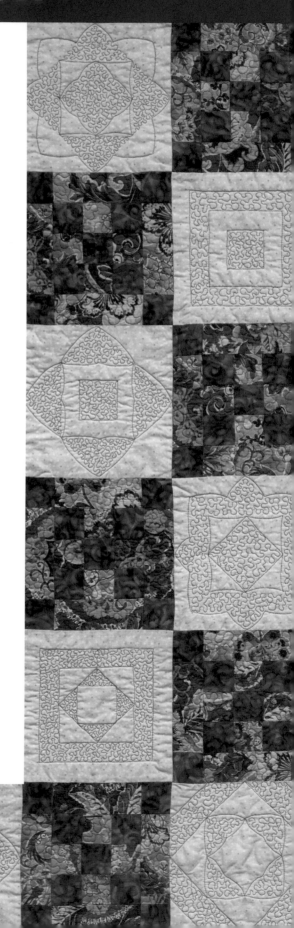

Getting Started

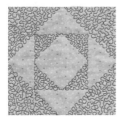

The following information outlines the supplies and preparations needed for free-motion quilting. Please take a moment to prepare your sewing machine and make sure you have everything you need before beginning.

SUPPLIES CHECKLIST

- Recently cleaned and serviced sewing machine and user's manual (see "Service Your Sewing Machine" at right)
- Sewing-machine extension table (optional, but highly recommended)
- Free-motion quilting foot
- Machine-quilting thread. You'll have fewer problems with thread breakage and a lot less lint in the bobbin, which can cause skipped stitches, if you use a high-quality thread. One of my personal favorites is Presencia machine-quilting thread, a three-ply, 100% mercerized long-staple Egyptian cotton thread. I use either a 40- or 50-weight thread, for both the top thread and the bobbin.
- New quilting needle. Quilting needles are stronger than normal sewing needles, and you'll be less likely to break one of these when free-motion quilting. I recommend Schmetz quilting needles, size 90/14.
- 1" x 12" clear acrylic ruler
- Fabric-marking pencils or pens in two colors. I love Pilot FriXion Ball Erasable Gel Pens. The ink is heat sensitive and can be removed with an iron. Wonderful!
- Quilting gloves (optional, but highly recommended). Quilting gloves can be any type of glove that helps you grip and move the fabric with less physical effort. I like Grabaroo's and Machingers. Both brands are made of nylon, so they're breathable while still form fitting. I think I'm starting to favor the Grabaroo's because I like to say their name and I love the bright purple color. It makes them easy to find!
- Paper and pencil (or pen) for drawing designs

Service Your Sewing Machine

Most quilters hate to spend money on stuff other than fabric, but getting your sewing machine serviced should be the exception to the rule. No matter how skilled you are in free-motion quilting, a machine in need of service will give you nothing but trouble. Treat yourself and have your machine serviced at least once a year.

PREPARE YOUR MACHINE

Running through the following checklist will ensure that your sewing machine is ready for a session of machine quilting.

- Attach the free-motion quilting foot in place of the regular presser foot.
- Thread the sewing machine with the same quilting thread in both the top and the bobbin.
- Drop the feed dogs. (If you're not sure how to do this, consult the user's manual for your sewing machine.)
- Put in a new quilting needle.
- Engage the needle-down function, if available. (Check your manual to find out whether your sewing machine has this option.)

THREAD BASICS

Thread is obviously an important part of the quilting process. Choosing the right color and type can spell the difference between success and disappointment.

Choosing a Thread Color

I like to decide how I'm going to quilt a finished top before I purchase my quilting thread. This way I know what color fabric I'll actually be quilting on and can get the best thread color to blend with it. It's simply a matter of auditioning the thread on the finished quilt top. I do this by unwinding about an arm's length of thread and laying it across the section I'm going to quilt. This shows me the true amount of contrast between the thread and the fabric. Free-motion quilting is never going to be absolutely perfect, and I don't want any "imperfect" spots to be overly obvious. The greater the contrast between the fabric and the thread, the more the stitching shows up. In most situations I want the texture of the design to be more noticeable than the thread color.

Matching the Top and Bobbin Threads

Thread tension can be a bit finicky for even the most experienced quilter. It's also natural for the tension to pop in and out of alignment while quilting (this even happens to long-arm quilters). Using the same weight and fiber content for both the top thread and the bobbin thread will make the tension easier to regulate and stabilize. Also, using the same color in the top and bobbin threads will better hide any variances in the thread-tension alignment.

Monofilament Thread

Many quilters like to use monofilament thread, which is semitransparent, to help hide imperfections in thread tension. However, I always caution new quilters about using it when they first start quilting. It's much harder to keep the tension balanced with monofilament because of its tendency to stretch. I highly recommend staying with a good cotton thread in both the top and the bobbin, and simply choosing a color that blends well with the fabric until you're comfortable adjusting your thread tension.

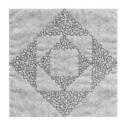

Many quilters are uncomfortable with free-motion quilting because they feel out of control with their technique. I felt the same way when I started. The problem for me was that I didn't know what to practice in order to improve. I needed something tangible to work on. Finally, after years of teaching free-motion quilting, I identified three specific areas you can focus on to improve your skills. I refer to them as the "free-motion basics." They are thread tension, stitch length, and quilting in smaller sections with frequent stops.

THREAD TENSION

Thread tension is the amount of strength needed for the top thread to pull the bobbin thread up to its proper position, which is in the middle of whatever is being sewn. *You'll know the tension is correct when quilting because the thread will be indented into the fabric and a "pillowing" effect will appear around the thread stitches on both the front and back of the quilt.* It's the result of both the top and bobbin threads being pulled into the middle of the batting.

The tension is correct when pillowing occurs around the stitches.

Problems with thread tension occur when we're quilting because of the thickness of the batting. The sewing machine's standard thread-tension setting is designed for sewing only two layers of fabric together. When quilting, the top thread tension is no longer strong enough to pull the bobbin thread into the middle of the batting. The tension is *too loose* and is the reason why you'll see the bobbin thread lying across the back of the quilt.

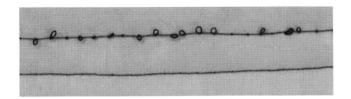

The first row of stitching shows where the tension is too loose and the black bobbin thread has been left lying on the back of the quilt instead of being pulled into the batting, as shown in the second row of stitching, where the thread tension has been tightened.

Most problems with thread tension are easily solved by increasing (or tightening) the tension. This is done by turning the upper-thread tension dial to a *higher number* in half-step increments. For example, if a machine's standard thread-tension setting is 4, start by setting the tension halfway between 4 and 5. Sew a test sample. If the thread is still lying on the back of the quilt, continue to increase the tension by half steps until both threads are pulled into the middle of the batting and the fabric pillows around the stitches. It's not unusual to increase the tension to as high as 6.5 or 7.

Where Is the Thread-Tension Dial?

Check your sewing-machine manual to make sure you are, in fact, adjusting the thread tension. For years I thought I was adjusting my thread tension, and it turned out I was adjusting the amount of pressure for my presser foot!

Testing Thread Tension

It's essential to test your thread tension before you start quilting each new project, because changes in fabric weight, batting thickness, and the type of thread used all affect the tension. I like to actually do my tension test on the side edge of the quilt I'm going to be free-motion quilting. I take a piece of the fabric I used in the quilt top, lay it on the extra backing and batting that extends past the quilt top, and practice on that.

An easy way to accurately test thread tension is by using the extra backing and batting on the side of the quilt with a piece of scrap fabric from the quilt top.

Exercise: How to Test Thread Tension

1. Thread the machine with the actual quilting thread to be used in the quilt.
2. Place the test section of the actual quilt under the needle and sew a line of stitches 3" to 4" long. If the stitches are too small to see clearly, sew another line of stitches with the machine running at a slower speed.
3. Remove the quilt from under the needle, clip the threads, and look at the thread tension on both the front and back of the sample area.
   - Is the fabric pillowing around the stitches? If it's not, the tension needs to be tightened (turned to a higher number).
   - Is the bobbin thread still lying on the back of the quilt? If it is, the tension needs to be increased quite a bit. You might need to make three to four changes in half-step increments before the tension is correct.
4. Continue testing and adjusting the tension settings in this manner until the tension is correct.

Monitoring the Tension

The thread tension on a sewing machine is fairly sensitive. It's easy to pull it out of alignment by moving the quilt too quickly as you're stitching. This usually happens when we start to relax and become more comfortable with our stippling design. That's why it's important to develop the habit of regularly looking at the back of the quilt about every 15 to 30 minutes to check the thread tension. I don't cut the threads or take the quilt out from under the machine; I just flip it over and look at the area closest to the needle to make sure the bobbin thread is being pulled into the batting to create the pillow effect, and that it's not pulling around the corners of the design. If you notice a problem and it's not too bad, tighten up the tension and resume quilting. Check it again after a few minutes to make sure the problem has been corrected. Keep in mind that it takes a lot longer to remove stitches than it does to quilt them. Trust me, I'm speaking from experience!

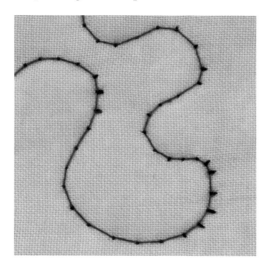

Tighten the tension to eliminate the bobbin thread from pulling around curves and corners of the design.

Variations among Machines

On some machines you need to raise the presser foot in order for a new tension setting to take effect. Check your user's manual to see if this pertains to your machine. If so, leave the needle down in the quilt, and then lift the presser foot to engage the new settings.

STITCH LENGTH

The desired stitch length for free-motion quilting is about ⅛", or eight stitches per inch. However, unless you have an actual stitch regulator for your sewing machine, it's impossible to make all the stitches exactly the same length. Our goal is for the *majority* of our stitches to be about ⅛" long.

I've found that the easiest way to control my stitch length is by focusing primarily on the *speed of the machine.* I like to think of the foot pedal of the sewing machine like the gas pedal of a car. If most of the stitches are shorter than ⅛", the machine needs to be slowed down—ease off the gas. If most of the stitches are longer than ⅛", the machine needs to go faster—give it more gas.

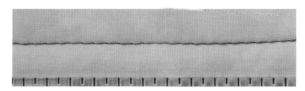

The majority of stitches are the right size, about ⅛" long.

The majority of stitches are shorter than ⅛". Ease off the gas pedal—slow down as you quilt.

The majority of stitches are longer than ⅛". Give the machine more gas— speed up as you quilt.

Check Stitch Length with Ruler

Develop the habit of actually measuring your stitch length with a ruler each time you start free-motion quilting. My students always roll their eyes at me when I suggest this, but it really does help you gain better control of your stitch length.

QUILTING IN SMALLER SECTIONS

The final topic of my free-motion quilting fundamentals involves quilting in smaller sections. This requires frequent stops, and I've found that most free-motion quilters don't like to pause or stop when stippling unless it's absolutely necessary. Unfortunately, failure to stop often enough is one of the primary reasons why quilters start to feel panicked and out of control with their stippling design. They try to quilt an area larger than their machine can handle and end up having to push and pull the quilt through the neck area of the machine while trying to figure out where to quilt next.

The ease with which you can move your quilt is the key to maintaining the design consistency and controlling the thread tension and stitch length. Most home sewing machines only have a neck opening that is about 5" to 6" wide. This means your quilting should stay focused on the 4½"-square area under the needle where there's room to move your quilt easily. This naturally lends itself to stopping frequently and repositioning both the quilt and your hands, which gives you that needed moment to relax and think about where to quilt next.

Hand Position

When free-motion quilting, it's important to frame the needle with your hands. This gives you greater control of your stitching by providing a better grip on the area you're quilting and keeping the fabric under the needle flat, which creates a smoother surface. Both of these things allow you to quilt with less effort, which ultimately makes you feel more comfortable and in control of your quilting.

Place your hands 2" to 3" from the needle, framing the quilting area.

My favorite way to frame the needle is with my right hand flat and my left hand grabbing the quilt. This position makes it easy for me to move the quilt.

QUILT POSITION

Quilting in smaller sections with frequent stops also makes it easier to manage the bulk of the quilt regardless of its size. This is because the only section that has to move at one time is the 4½"-square area under the needle. The rest of the quilt just needs to be supported so it's not pulling and making it difficult to maneuver the section being worked on.

Here's how I do it:

1. Make sure there's enough space around the sewing machine to lay the quilt out without it catching on something or falling to the floor. I quilt on an old dining-room table with a lightweight rolling cart pulled close to my left side. This provides support on all sides of the quilt.

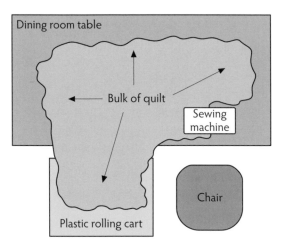

2. Position the section to be worked on under the needle.
3. Fluff the quilt and make sure the 4½"-square area under the needle can move easily in all directions. If at any time it becomes hard to shift in a certain direction, the quilt is probably caught on something and needs to be fluffed again.
4. Quilt the area.
5. Continue to the next 4½"-square section that needs to be quilted and repeat the fluffing process.

Stippling Simplified

Stippling is one of the most popular styles of free-motion quilting. It's free-form meandering design makes it a quick and easy way to finish a quilt while adding great texture. New quilters usually want to learn and master it as quickly as possible but tend to become frustrated when they can't figure out how to reproduce the meandering "look."

I felt this way when I was trying to learn to stipple. The helpful hint I was given after my first class was to be patient and remember that "it just takes practice." My question was, "How can I practice something I don't know how to do?" That's why my goal when I started teaching stippling was to break down the design into something anyone could relate to and draw. What I discovered was the design was simply a series of "wiggles."

COMPONENTS OF A WIGGLE

A wiggle is made up of two "hills" and a "valley." Each hill is simply three-quarters of a circle. The "hills" are connected by a "valley," which is a dip that connects the circles. The combination of the two creates an up-down-up-down motion, also

thought of as a 1-2-3-4 pattern, which is the foundation of the stippling design.

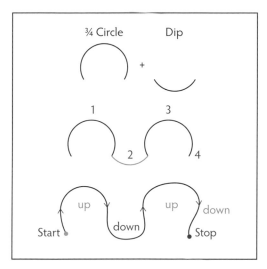

Wiggle = ¾ Circle + Dip + ¾ Circle

The wiggle is stitched the same way regardless of the size of the stippling design. It's always a 1-2-3-4 pattern.

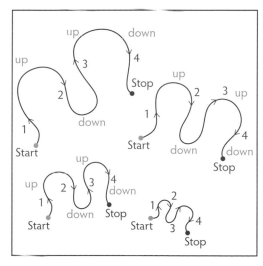

Stippling design is a 4-part pattern

The direction in which the wiggle is stitched (up-down-up-down, down-up-down-up, or side to side) will need to change based on the area that is being filled in with stippling, but the 1-2-3-4 pattern stays the same.

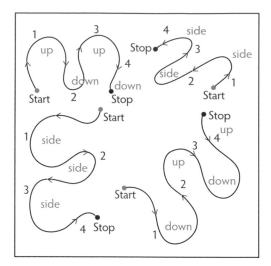

Wiggles drawn in different directions

The wiggles are connected by an additional dip to create the stippling design. This extra dip not only connects the wiggles but also allows you to change directions. The length of the dips will vary based on where you need to put the next wiggle to fill in the area you're stippling.

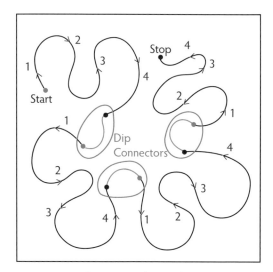

Connecting the wiggles

As I've said, stippling is a free-form design. The size, shape, and length of the wiggles and dips are supposed to be different. We need to change our view of stippling from creating the perfect design to using the meandering pattern to help us fill in the area we're quilting. If you need to move to the left, you add a dip in that direction. If you need to fill in a corner, then you make a hill or valley longer to fill it in. If you have a longer distance to travel between wiggles, you simply stretch out the dip. The key is to stay consistent with the 1-2-3-4 pattern.

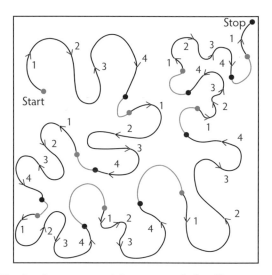

Wiggles change size and shape as needed to fill in an area.

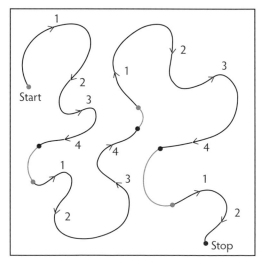

The 1-2-3-4 pattern is consistent regardless of the wiggle size and shape.

Stippling Simplified

It's *much harder* to maintain the stippling design when you're focusing on filling in an area larger than 4½" square. The design starts to flatten out, turning into straight lines of stitching with occasional bumps. This usually happens because the quilter is trying to push and pull the quilt around in order to quilt the larger area without stopping. This puts extra pressure on the quilter, and he or she tends to lose control of not only the design but also the thread tension and stitch length.

Stippling Designs Gone Wrong

Long lines of straight stitches are what kill most stippling designs. Always wiggle when moving to different areas. The greater the height and depth of the wiggles, the better they look.

Another way to maintain consistency when stippling is to think about how you're going to fill in an area before you start moving. I tend to follow one of two general paths when quilting. I use a down-up-down stitching path when quilting 4½" square areas, and I use a back-and-forth stitching path when quilting a smaller area. By consistently following these paths, I can relax because I know where I'm going and don't have to worry about stitching myself into a corner.

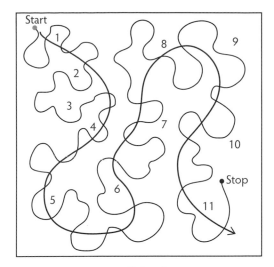

Put it all together.

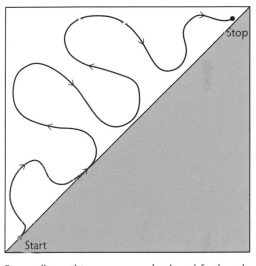

For smaller quilting areas use a back-and-forth path.

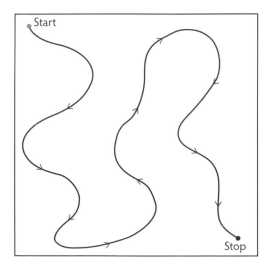

For larger quilting areas, use a down-up-down stitching path.

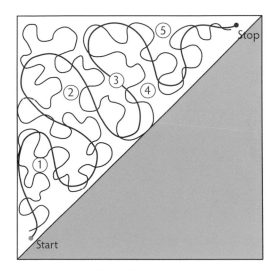

Put it all together.

FIVE WAYS TO IMPROVE STIPPLING SKILLS

You can instantly improve your stippling skills by using my five surefire tips for better machine quilting.

1. **Draw the stippling design.** I've found that if I can comfortably and consistently draw a design on paper, the design becomes a lot easier to quilt. It usually doesn't take more than a few minutes to get back into the flow of the design. Remember, stippling is a free-form technique—there is no right or wrong design.

2. **Stop often.** As soon as you sense that "panicked" or out-of-control feeling, stop and take the time to look ahead at the area you're working on. By thinking calmly about where you need to quilt next, you'll be able to continue stippling with greater focus and control.

3. **Keep your hands surrounding the needle.** Your hands should frame the needle by being about 2½" from either side of it. This gives you optimum control of the design and keeps the fabric flat for smoother quilting.

4. **Don't slide your hands.** Don't get lazy and try to reposition your hands and the quilt while running the machine. Establish the habit of stopping the machine, and then moving your hands.

5. **Wear quilting gloves.** I can't quilt without them. They give me a better grip on the fabric, which allows me to relax and use less effort to move the quilt. This also keeps my neck and shoulders from getting tight.

Solving Mysterious Thread Problems

All of us have experienced this at some point: We're quilting along and all of a sudden the bobbin thread is a mess on the back of the quilt, the machine starts eating the thread, or the thread keeps breaking. It never seems to make any sense as to why it's happening.

The good news is, about 90% of the time when this has happened to me, I've been able to fix the problem by simply rethreading the machine. I can't explain why it works, but it does. The key when rethreading the machine is to *completely* redo it.

1. Cut the top thread and take the top thread spool *all the way* off the sewing machine. Put the spool back on the machine and rethread it.

2. Take the bobbin out of the bobbin case and put it back in, making sure the thread goes through the bobbin-case tension guide.

The Design Mechanics

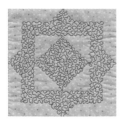 Once you understand the basics of free-motion quilting and stippling, you're ready to move on to the fun part—the quilting designs. My belief has always been that a good quilting design doesn't have to be complicated or intricate to be interesting and effective. The designs in this book can all be marked in less than two minutes and were created specifically to be stitched by the everyday quilter on a home sewing machine. They take into consideration the limited space available (4½") around the needle and are broken into manageable segments to encourage frequent stopping.

All of the designs are based on one of six different frame styles, which are created from the same basic set of reference lines. Each frame can be used on its own, with beautiful results, but you can also add one of the four filler designs. Outline stitching can then be added to the frame and/or filler. Each element adds a unique texture and gives the frame a different look. The design choices are limitless. You control how much detail to include and how much time to invest, simply by the amount of options you add.

Let's start by looking at the different frames and fillers. You'll learn how to mark the basic reference lines on your blocks, and I'll explain outline stitching. From there we'll delve into the step-by-step instructions for stitching the frames, plus you'll see options for combining the frames with fillers and outline stitching.

Frames

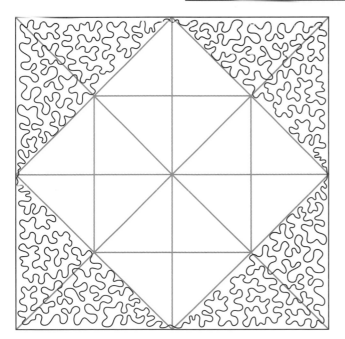

Four Corners Frame.

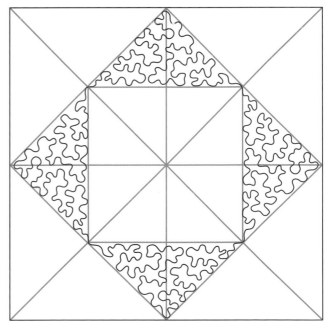

Four Triangles Frame.

Double Diamond Frame.

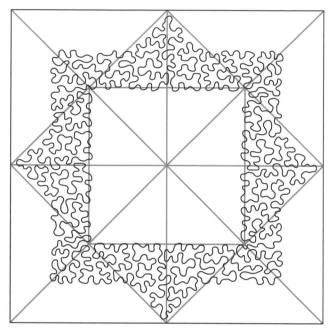

Star Frame.

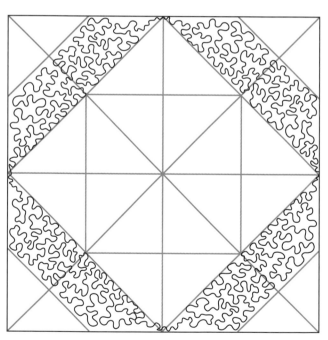

Half-Corners Frame.

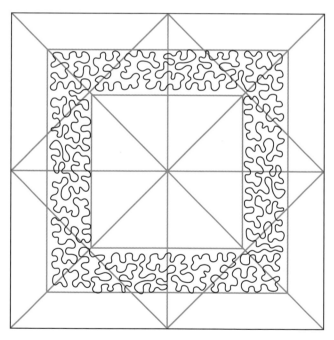

Inside Border Frame.

The Design Mechanics

Solid Diamond Filler.

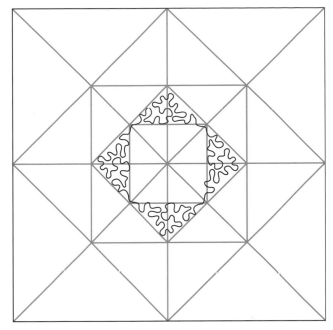

Open Diamond Filler.

Open Square Filler.

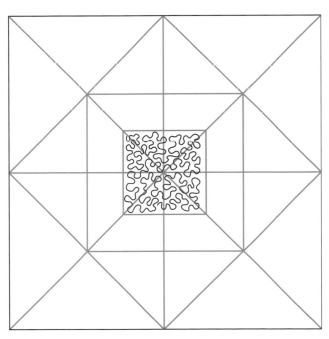

Solid Square Filler.

MARKING THE REFERENCE LINES

All of the designs are created by marking a quilt block with a set of basic reference lines. These reference lines are what enable you to quilt the designs with such ease. They show you the center of the block and evenly divide it into manageable sections. The frames and fillers are then created by using stippling to fill in different sections formed by the lines.

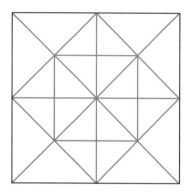

Basic Reference Lines.

The reference lines can be marked on any size or shape of block, such as a diamond or rectangle, as well as setting triangles, which are simply half of a block.

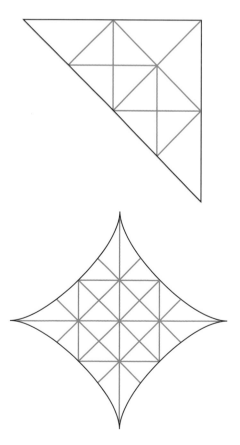

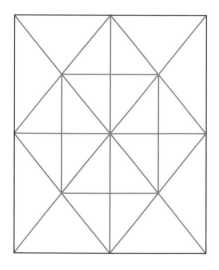

An additional benefit of the basic reference lines is that they give you actual lines to quilt on and logical places to stop. As I mentioned before, stopping frequently will allow you to relax and have more consistency and control over your quilting design, as well as your stitch length and thread tension.

Drawing the Basic Reference Lines

1. **Mark the diagonal, horizontal, and vertical lines.** Draw diagonal lines from each corner of the quilt block (red). Use the intersection of the diagonal lines to mark horizontal and vertical lines (blue).

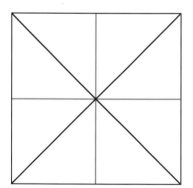

The Design Mechanics

2. Draw the outer diamond. Mark and connect reference points at the endpoints of the horizontal and vertical lines to form the outer diamond (red).

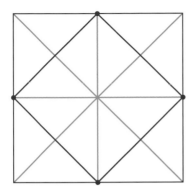

3. Draw the inner square. Mark the midpoint on each side of the outer diamond and connect them to form an inner square (red).

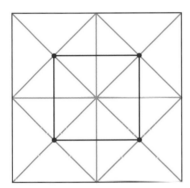

Marking Additional Reference Lines
These additional reference lines are only used for some of the frame and filler designs.

Midpoint of the inner square's sides. Mark and connect the midpoints to form an additional diamond (red).

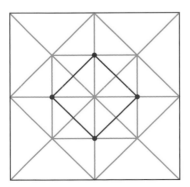

Midpoint of the inner square's diagonal lines. Mark and connect these midpoints to form the outer edge of the solid square filler (red).

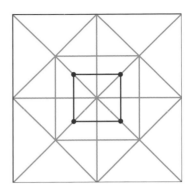

Midpoint of the grid's outer-corner diagonal lines. These midpoints (red) are used to create the outside edge for the inner border, star, and half-triangle frames.

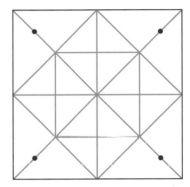

All at Once or One at a Time?

You can mark the reference lines one quilt block at a time or do them all at once. Personally, I find it easier to mark them all at once.

ADDING OUTLINE STITCHING

Outline stitching is another detail you can add to the design. The stitching can be done with either straight or curved lines and can be used on the frame, the filler, or both the frame and filler.

Straight and curved outline stitching on the same design

Just as with stitching the frames and fillers, the key to successful outline stitching—whether straight or curved—is to stop often and reposition your hands. Doing so gives you much more control and keeps the stitching smooth.

Straight Outline Stitching

The great thing about straight outline stitching is that the stitching line has already been drawn onto the block and all you have to do is follow it. Here are some hints for keeping your stitches straight.

Keep your eyes on the needle. It's easier to stitch on the drawn lines if you keep your eyes focused directly on the needle.

Make gradual corrections. If you veer off the stitching line, make your adjustments gradually and they will be less noticeable.

Stop often. You can keep the section being quilted framed with your hands if you stop often. (Note: Make sure your needle-down function is engaged.)

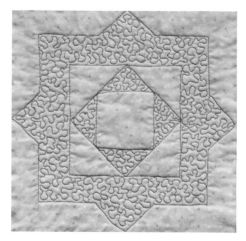

Straight outline stitching on both the frame and the filler

Curved Outline Stitching

I love the texture created by curved outline stitching. Each curve is simply half of an oval shape, created by stitching from midpoint to midpoint on the frame's or filler's edge. You'll find some hints for consistent curves on page 25.

Curved outline stitching on the outside of the frame and filler design

Keep the stitching close to the frame and/ or filler. The curves look more consistent when they're shallow and close to the section they're outlining. The deeper the curve, the more noticeable variations will be.

Keep line segments short. Lines of stitching over 2" long are harder to keep consistent in shape. If the section is over 3" it should be divided in half. The midpoints of the frame and filler sides are usually the best place to split the segment.

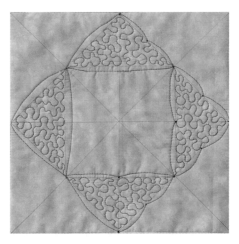

Half of the block was sewn with shorter line segments and the other half was sewn with longer line segments, which are harder to stitch consistently.

Use low-contrast thread color. The greater the contrast between the thread color and the fabric, the more the stitch "imperfections" show up. This is another reason to wait to purchase your thread until you've decided on which design you'll use on the quilt top.

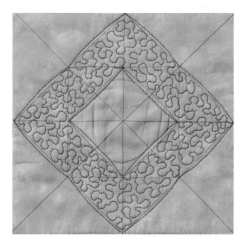

Different widths of curved outline stitching

Combining Elements for Fantastic Designs

At first glance, marking the reference lines for the designs can seem a bit overwhelming. Don't worry! It's just a matter of following the instructions one step at a time.

1. Start by deciding which frame or frame-and-filler design you want to stitch.
2. Select an outline stitching option from those shown after each design, if desired.
3. Once you've decided on the design elements (filler and outline stitching), mark the basic reference lines (refer to "Marking the Reference Lines" on page 22).
4. Mark any additional reference lines as instructed. For additional ease, I've color coded the lines you'll be using on the illustrations, with appropriate references in the written instructions.
5. After marking the reference lines, identify the specific lines that will be used to create the design, as indicated in the instructions. I find it helpful to lightly shade in the sections on the quilt block that will create the frame and filler. It makes it easier for me to see where I'm going to quilt. These sections are shown in gray on the illustrations.

Frame and filler design shaded in on the quilt block

The instructions are written for continuous free-motion quilting, so you don't need to cut and trim the threads until instructed.

Four Corners Frame

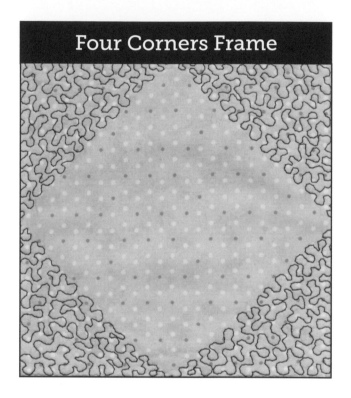

1. Identify the outer diamond and the inner square (red). Shade in the sections to be stitched, if desired.

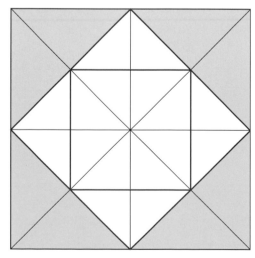

Mark reference lines.

2. If you're not outline stitching the frame, skip to step 3. If you're adding outline stitching, start at one corner of the outer diamond and outline stitch the frame's inner edge. Leave the needle down at the stopping point.

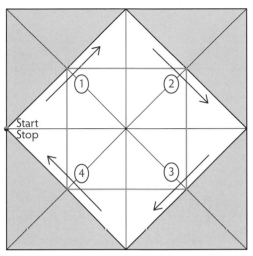

Outline stitch frame.

3. Start at one corner of the outer diamond (or at the point where you stopped outline stitching) and fill in the frame design with stippling, moving from one section to another by stitching over the corners. Secure and trim the threads.

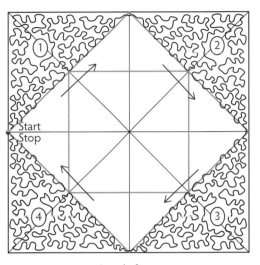

Stipple frame.

Outlining Options

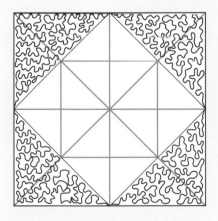 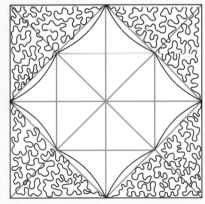

Four Corners Frame and Solid Diamond Filler

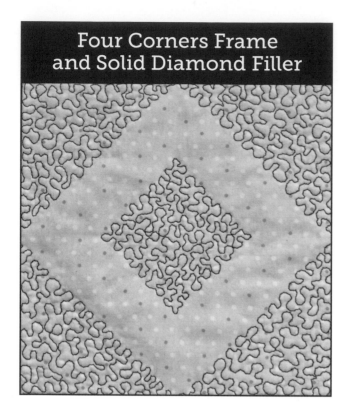

2. If you're not outline stitching the filler, skip to step 3. If you're adding outline stitching, start at one of the filler's corner points and outline stitch the outer edge. Leave the needle down at the stopping point.

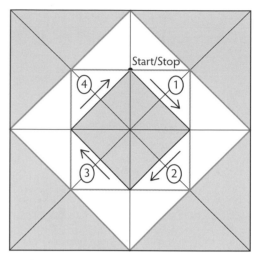

Outline stitch filler.

1. Identify the outer diamond and the inner square (red). Mark and connect the midpoints of the inner square's sides to form the filler's outside edge (blue). Shade in the sections to be stitched, if desired.

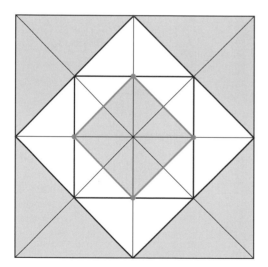

Mark reference lines.

3. Start at one of the filler's corner points (or at the point where you stopped outline stitching) and stipple the inside of the filler. Exit the design at the opposite corner. Secure and trim the threads.

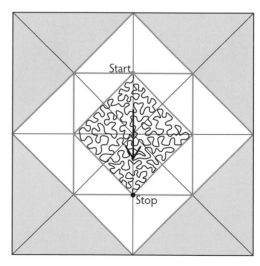

Stipple filler.

4. If you're not outline stitching the frame, skip to step 5. If you're adding outline stitching, start at one corner of the outer diamond and outline stitch the frame's inner edge. Leave the needle down at the stopping point.

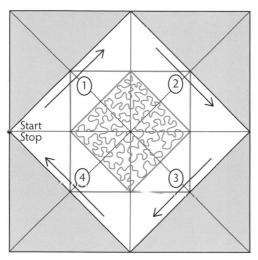

Outline stitch frame.

5. Start at one corner of the outer diamond (or at the point where you stopped outline stitching) and fill in the frame design with stippling, moving from one section to another by stitching over the corners. Secure and trim the threads.

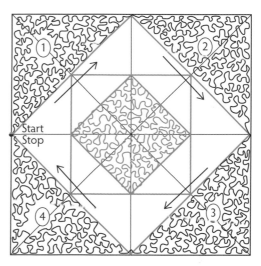

Stipple frame.

Outlining Options

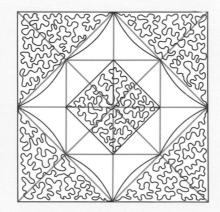

Four Corners Frame and Open Square Filler

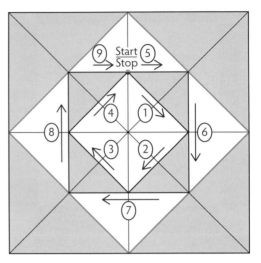

1. Identify the outer diamond and the inner square (red). Mark and connect the midpoints of the inner square's sides to form the filler's inner edge (blue). Shade in the sections to be stitched, if desired.

Mark reference lines.

2. If you're not outline stitching the filler, skip to step 3. If you're adding outline stitching, start at one midpoint of the inner square and outline stitch the filler's inner and outer edges. Leave the needle down at the stopping point.

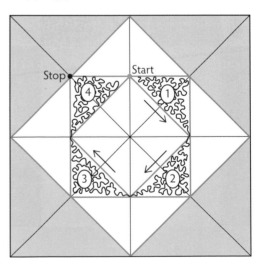

Outline stitch filler.

3. Start at one of the inner square's midpoints (or at the point where you stopped outline stitching) and stipple the inside of each filler section, moving from one section to another by stitching over the corners. Exit the last section where it touches the frame. Leave the needle down at the stopping point.

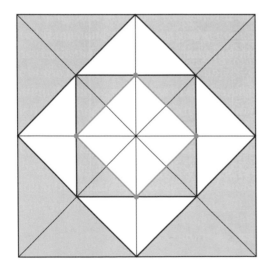

Stipple filler.

4. If you're not outline stitching the frame, skip to step 5. If you're adding outline stitching, continue stitching and outline stitch the frame's inner edge. Leave the needle down at the stopping point.

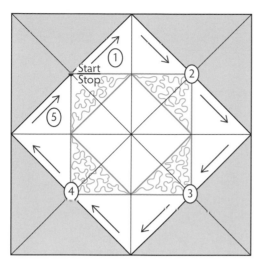

Outline stitch frame.

5. Continue stitching from where you had stopped and fill in the frame design with stippling, moving from one section to another by stitching over the corners. Secure and trim the threads.

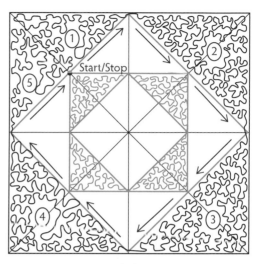

Stipple frame.

Combining Elements for Fantastic Designs

Outlining Options

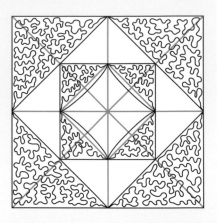

Combining Elements for Fantastic Designs

Four Corners Frame and Open Diamond Filler

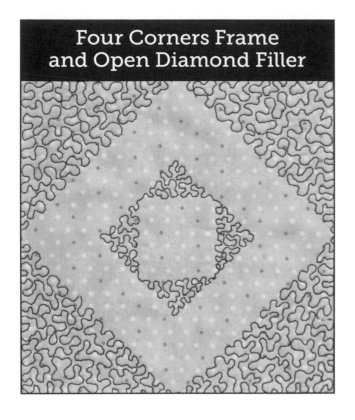

2. If you're not outline stitching the filler, skip to step 3. If you're adding outline stitching, start at one of the filler's side midpoints and outline stitch its inner and outer edges. Leave the needle down at the stopping point.

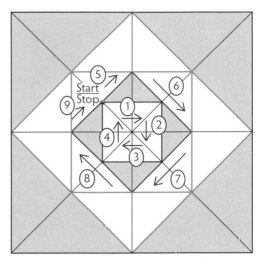

Outline stitch filler.

1. Identify the outer diamond and the inner square (red). Mark and connect the midpoints of the inner square's sides to form the filler's outer edge (blue). Mark and connect the midpoints of the filler's outer edge to form the filler's inner edge (green). Shade in the sections to be stitched, if desired.

3. Start at one of the filler's side midpoints (or at the point where you stopped outline stitching) and stipple the inside of each filler section, moving from one section to another by stitching over the corners. Secure and trim the threads.

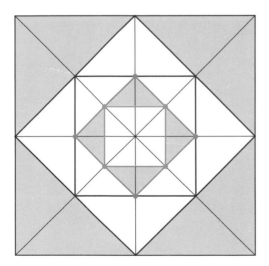

Mark reference lines.

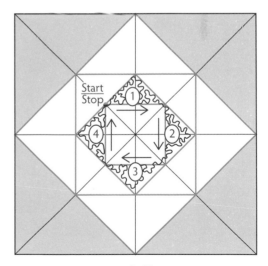

Stipple filler.

4. If you're not outline stitching the frame, skip to step 5. If you're adding outline stitching, start at one corner of the outer diamond and outline stitch the frame's inner edge. Leave the needle down at the stopping point.

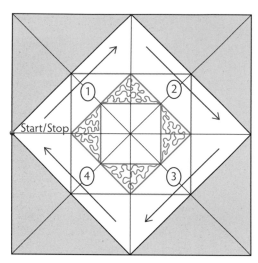

Outline stitch frame.

5. Start at one corner of the outer diamond (or at the point where you stopped outline stitching) and fill in the frame design with stippling, moving from one section to another by stitching over the corners. Secure and trim the threads.

Stipple the frame.

Combining Elements for Fantastic Designs

Outlining Options

Four Triangles Frame

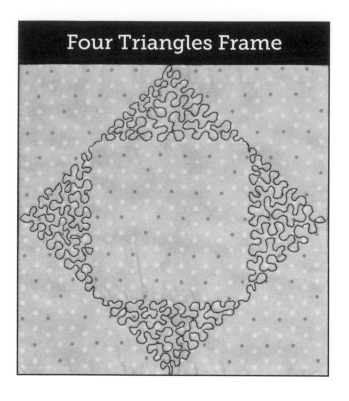

1. Identify the outer diamond and the inner square (red). Shade in the section to be stitched, if desired.

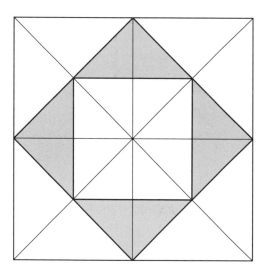

Mark reference lines.

2. If you're not outline stitching the frame, skip to step 3. If you're adding outline stitching, start at one corner of the inner square and outline stitch the frame's inner and outer edges. Leave the needle down at the stopping point.

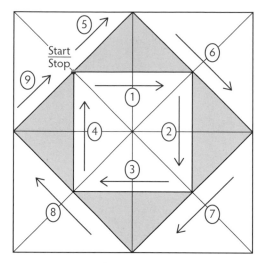

Outline stitch frame.

3. Start at one corner of the inner square (or at the point where you stopped outline stitching) and fill in the frame design with stippling, moving from one section to another by stitching over the corners. Secure and trim the threads.

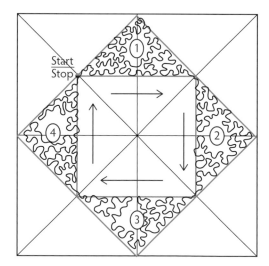

Stipple frame.

Combining Elements for Fantastic Designs

Outlining Options

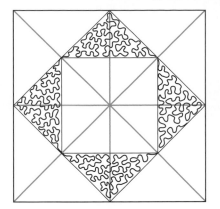

Four Triangles Frame and Solid Diamond Filler

1. Identify the outer diamond and the inner square (red). Mark and connect the midpoints of the inner square's sides to form the filler's outer edge (blue). Shade in the sections to be stitched, if desired.

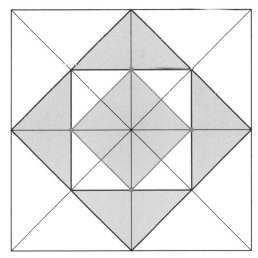

Mark reference lines.

2. If you're not outline stitching the filler, skip to step 3. If you're adding outline stitching, start at one of the filler's corner points and outline stitch the filler's outside edge. Leave the needle down at the stopping point.

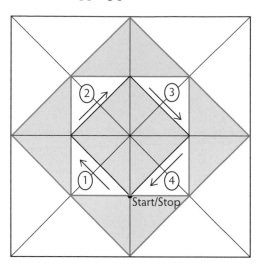

Outline stitch filler.

3. Start at one of the filler's corner points (or at the point where you stopped outline stitching) and stipple the inside of the filler. Exit the design at the opposite corner where it touches the frame. Leave the needle down at the stopping point.

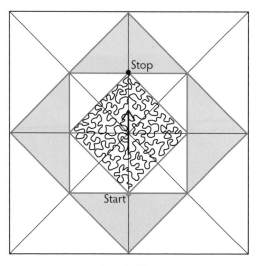

Stipple filler.

4. If you're not outline stitching the frame, skip to step 5. If you're adding outline stitching, continue stitching and outline stitch the frame's inner edge. Move inside the frame and stipple up to the outer edge of the design (5). Outline stitch the frame's outer edge. Leave the needle down at the stopping point.

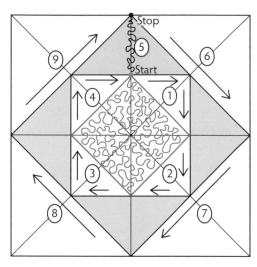

Outline stitch frame.

5. Continue stitching and fill in the frame design with stippling, moving from one section to another by stitching over the corners. Secure and trim the threads.

Stipple frame.

Outlining Options

Combining Elements for Fantastic Designs

Four Triangles Frame and Open Diamond Filler

1. Identify the outer diamond and the inner square (red). Mark and connect the midpoints of the inner square's sides to form the filler's outer edge (blue). Mark and connect the midpoints of the filler's outer edge to form the filler's inner edge (green). Shade in the sections to be stitched, if desired.

Mark reference lines.

2. If you're not outline stitching the filler, skip to step 3. If you're adding outline stitching, start at one of the filler's side midpoints and outline stitch the inner and outer edges. Leave the needle down at the stopping point.

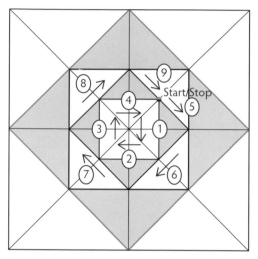

Outline stitch filler.

3. Start at one of the filler's side midpoints (or at the point where you stopped outline stitching) and stipple the inside of each filler section, moving from one section to another by stitching over the corners. Exit the section where it touches the frame. Leave the needle down at the stopping point.

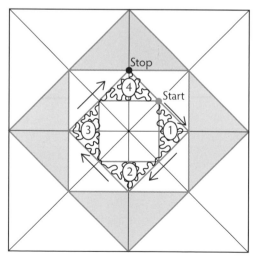

Stipple filler.

Combining Elements for Fantastic Designs

4. If you're not outline stitching the frame, skip to step 5. If you're adding outline stitching, continue stitching and outline stitch the frame's inner edge. Move inside the frame and stipple up to the outer edge of the design. Outline stitch the frame's outer edge. Leave the needle down at the stopping point.

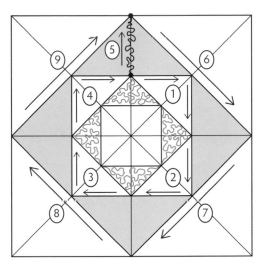

Outline stitch frame.

5. Continue stitching and fill in the frame design with stippling, moving from one section to another by stitching over the corners. Secure and trim the threads.

Stipple frame.

Outlining Options

Combining Elements for Fantastic Designs

Four Triangles Frame and Solid Square Filler

2. If you're not outline stitching the filler, skip to step 3. If you're adding outline stitching, start at one of the filler's corners and outline stitch the filler's outer edge. Leave the needle down at the stopping point.

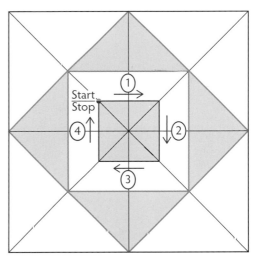

Outline stitch filler.

1. Identify the outer diamond and the inner square (red). Mark and connect the midpoints of the inner square's diagonal lines to form the fillers outer edge (blue). Shade in the sections to be stitched, if desired.

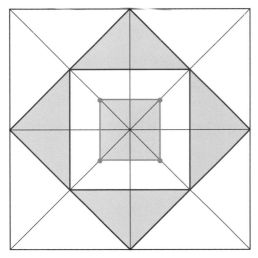

Mark reference lines.

3. Start at one of the filler's corners (or at the point where you stopped outline stitching) and stipple the inside of the filler. Exit the section at the opposite corner. Secure and trim the threads.

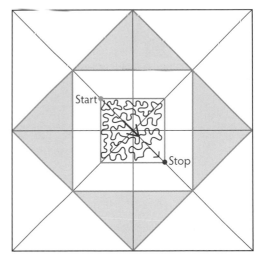

Stipple filler.

4. If you're not outline stitching the frame, skip to step 5. If you're adding outline stitching, start at one of the inner square's corners and outline stitch the frame's inner and outer edges. Leave the needle down at the stopping point.

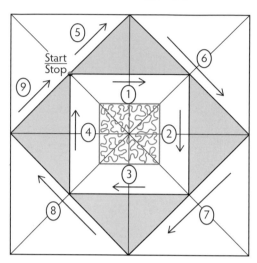

Outline stitch frame.

5. Start at one of the inner square's corners (or at the point where you stopped outline stitching) and fill in the frame design with stippling, moving from one section to another by stitching over the corners. Secure and trim the threads.

Stipple frame.

Combining Elements for Fantastic Designs

Outlining Options

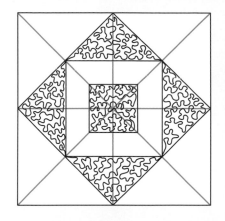

Combining Elements for Fantastic Designs

Double Diamond Frame

2. If you're not outline stitching the frame, skip to step 3. If you're adding outline stitching, start at one of the inner square's midpoints and outline stitch the frame's inner edge. Move inside the frame and stipple up to the outer edge of the frame. Outline stitch the frame's outer edge. Leave the needle down at the stopping point.

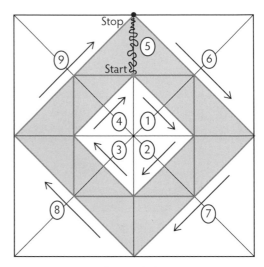

Outline stitch frame.

1. Identify the outer diamond and the inner square (red). Mark and connect the midpoints of the inner square's sides (blue). Shade in the section to be stitched, if desired.

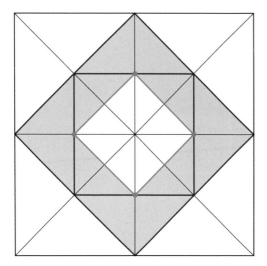

Mark reference lines.

3. Start at one of the inner square's midpoints (or at the point where you stopped outline stitching) and fill in the frame design with stippling. Secure and trim the threads.

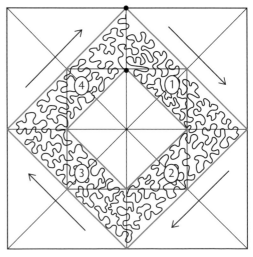

Stipple frame.

Combining Elements for Fantastic Designs

Outlining Options

Star Frame

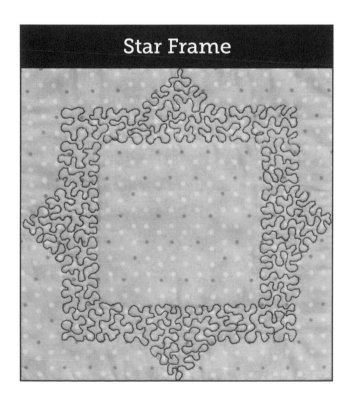

1. Identify the outer diamond and the inner square (red). Mark the midpoint of the diagonal line on each of the outer corners (blue). Connect these midpoints to the edges of the outer diamond to create the corners of the frame (blue). Shade in the sections to be stitched, if desired.

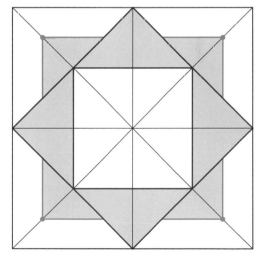

Mark reference lines.

2. If you're not outline stitching the frame, skip to step 3. If you're adding outline stitching, start at one corner of the inner square and outline stitch the frame's inside edge. Move inside the frame and stipple up to the outer edge of the frame (5). Outline stitch the frame's outer edge. Leave the needle down at the stopping point.

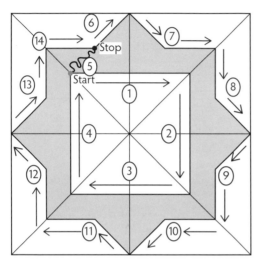

Outline stitch frame.

3. Start at one corner of the inside square (or at the point where you stopped outline stitching) and fill in the frame design with stippling. Secure and trim the threads.

Stipple frame.

Outlining Options

Combining Elements for Fantastic Designs

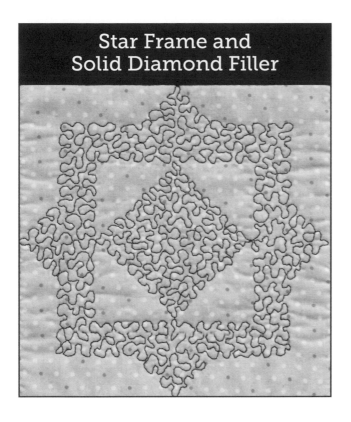

Star Frame and Solid Diamond Filler

2. If you're not outline stitching the filler, skip to step 3. If you're adding outline stitching, start at one of the filler's corner points and outline stitch the filler's outer edge. Leave the needle down at the stopping point.

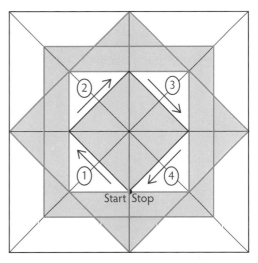

Outline stitch filler.

1. Identify the outer diamond and the inner square (red). Mark the midpoint of the diagonal line on each outer corner (blue). Connect these midpoints to the edges of the outer diamond to create the corners of the frame (blue). Mark and connect the midpoints of the inner square's sides to form the filler's outer edge (green). Shade in the sections to be stitched, if desired.

3. Start at one of the filler's corner points (or at the point where you stopped outline stitching) and stipple the inside of the filler. Exit the design at the opposite corner where it touches the frame. Leave the needle down at the stopping point.

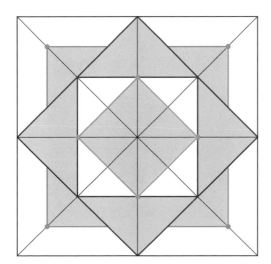

Mark reference lines.

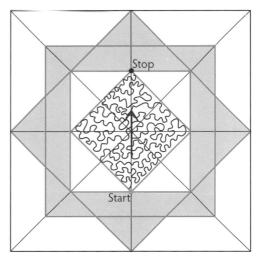

Stipple filler.

4. If you're not outline stitching the frame, skip to step 5. If you're adding outline stitching, outline stitch the frame's inner edge. Move inside the frame and stipple up to the outer edge of the design (5). Outline stitch the frame's outer edge. Leave the needle down at the stopping point.

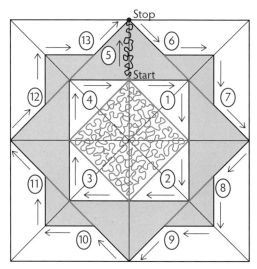

Outline stitch frame.

5. Continue stitching and fill in the frame design with stippling. Secure and trim the threads.

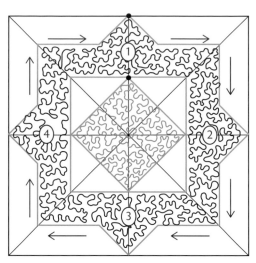

Stipple frame.

Combining Elements for Fantastic Designs

Outlining Options

Combining Elements for Fantastic Designs

Star Frame and Open Diamond Filler

2. If you're not outline stitching the filler, skip to step 3. If you're adding outline stitching, start at one of the filler's side midpoints and outline stitch the inner and outer edges. Leave the needle down at the stopping point.

Outline stitch filler.

1. Identify the outer diamond and the inner square (red). Mark the midpoint of the diagonal line on each outer corner (blue). Connect these midpoints to the edges of the outer diamond to create the corners of the frame (blue). Mark and connect the midpoints of the inner square's sides to form the filler's outer edge (green). Mark and connect the midpoints of the filler's outer edge to form the filler's inner edge (orange). Shade in the sections to be stitched, if desired.

3. Start at one of the filler's side midpoints (or at the point where you stopped outline stitching) and stipple the inside of each filler section, moving from one section to another by stitching over the corners. Exit the last section where it touches the frame. Leave the needle down at the stopping point.

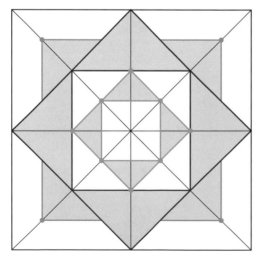

Mark reference lines.

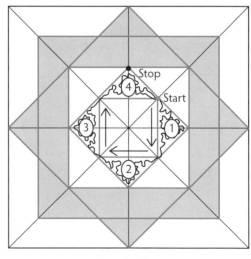

Stipple filler.

4. If you're not outline stitching the frame, skip to step 5. If you're adding outline stitching, outline stitch the frame's inside edge. Move inside the frame and stipple up to the outside edge of the design (5). Outline stitch the frame's outside edge. Leave the needle down at the stopping point.

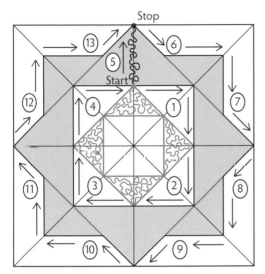

Outline stitch frame.

5. Continue stitching and fill in the frame design with stippling. Secure and trim the threads.

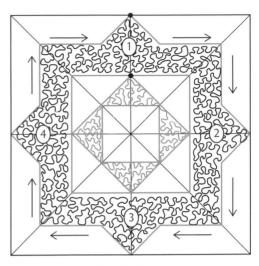

Stipple frame.

Outlining Options

Combining Elements for Fantastic Designs

Star Frame and Solid Square Filler

1. Identify the outer diamond and the inner square (red). Mark the midpoint of the diagonal line on each outer corner (blue). Connect these midpoints to the edges of the outer diamond to create the corners of the frame (blue). Mark and connect the midpoints of the inner square's diagonal lines to form the filler's outer edge (green). Shade in the sections to be stitched, if desired.

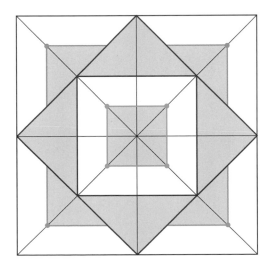

Mark reference lines.

2. If you're not outline stitching the filler, skip to step 3. If you're adding outline stitching, start at one of the filler's corners and outline stitch the filler's outer edge. Leave the needle down at the stopping point.

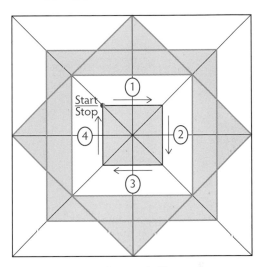

Outline stitch filler.

3. Start at one of the filler's corners (or at the point where you stopped outline stitching) and stipple the inside of the filler, exiting the design at the opposite corner. Secure and trim the threads.

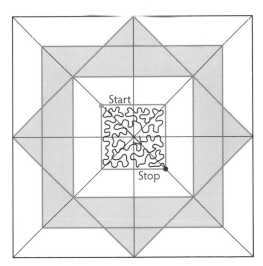

Stipple filler.

4. If you're not outline stitching the frame, skip to step 5. If you're adding outline stitching, start at one of the inner square's corners and outline stitch the frame's inner edge. Move inside the frame and stipple up to the outer edge of the design (5). Outline stitch the frame's outer edge. Leave the needle down at the stopping point.

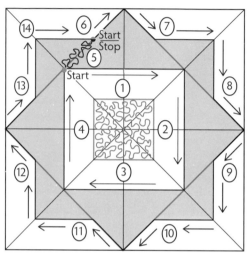

Outline stitch frame.

5. Start at one of the inner square's corners (or at the point you stopped stitching) and fill in the frame design with stippling. Secure and trim the threads.

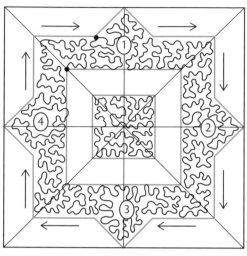

Stipple frame.

Combining Elements for Fantastic Designs

Outlining Options

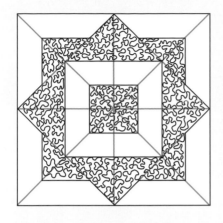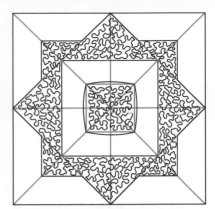

Combining Elements for Fantastic Designs

Half-Corners Frame

1. Identify the outer diamond and inside square (red). Mark the midpoint of the diagonal line on each outer corner (blue). Use the midpoints to draw a line parallel to each side of the outer diamond to form the frame's outer edge (blue). Shade in the sections to be stitched, if desired.

Mark reference lines.

2. If you're not outline stitching the frame, skip to step 5. If you're adding outline stitching, start at one corner of the outer diamond and outline stitch the frame's inner edge. Move inside the frame and stipple up to the outer edge of the design (5).

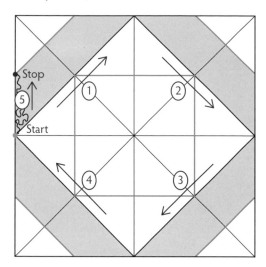

Outline stitch frame.

3. Outline stitch one section of the frame's outer diagonal edge. Move back inside the frame and fill the section with stippling, moving to the next area by stitching over the corner.

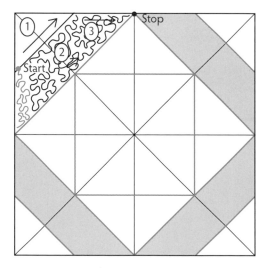

Outline stitch and then stipple first area of frame.

Combining Elements for Fantastic Designs

4. Continue around the frame, outline stitching each diagonal edge and then filling in the section with stippling. Secure and trim the threads.

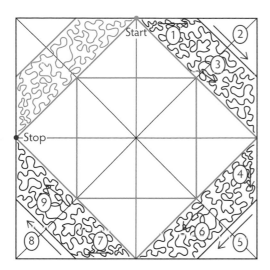

Continue outline stitching and stippling remaining areas of frame.

5. If you're not outline stitching, start stitching at one corner of the outer square and fill in the frame design with stippling, moving from one section to another by stitching over the corners. Secure and trim the threads.

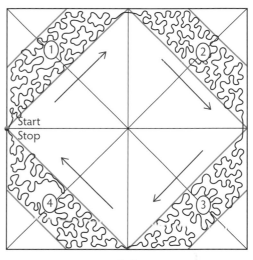

Stipple frame.

Outlining Options

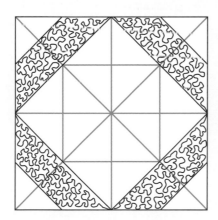 

Half-Corners Frame and Open Square Filler

2. If you're not outline stitching the filler, skip to step 3. If you're adding outline stitching, start at one of the inner square's midpoints and outline stitch the filler's inner and outer edges. Leave the needle down at the stopping point.

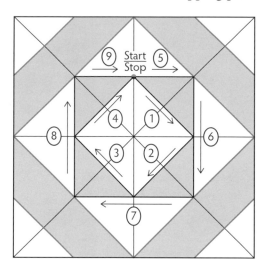

Outline stitch filler.

1. Identify the outer diamond and the inner square (red). Mark the midpoint of the diagonal line on each outer corner (blue). Use the midpoints to draw a line parallel to each side of the outer diamond to form the frame's outside edge (blue). Mark and connect the midpoints of the inner square's sides to form the filler's inner edge (green). Shade in the sections to be stitched, if desired.

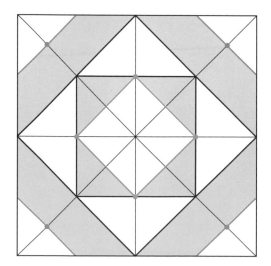

Mark reference lines.

3. Start at one of the inner square's midpoints (or at the point where you stopped outline stitching) and stipple the inside of each filler section, moving from one section to another by stitching over the corners. Exit the last section where it touches the frame. Leave the needle down at the stopping point.

Stipple filler.

4. If you're not outline stitching the frame, skip to step 7. If you're adding outline stitching, continue stitching and outline stitch the frame's inner edge. Move inside the frame and stipple up to the outer edge of the design (6).

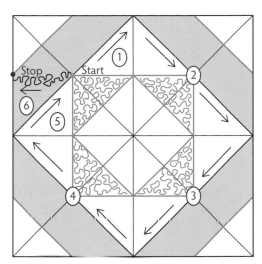

Outline stitch frame's inner edge.

5. Outline stitch one section of the frame's outer diagonal edge. Move back inside the frame and fill it with stippling, moving to the next section by stitching over the corner.

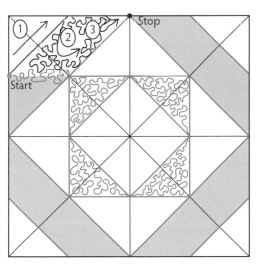

Outline stitch and then stipple first area of frame.

6. Continue around the frame, outline stitching each diagonal edge of the frame and then filling in the section with stippling. Secure and trim the threads.

Continue outline stitching and stippling remaining areas of frame.

7. If you're not outline stitching, continue stitching and fill in each section of the frame design with stippling, moving from one section to another by stitching over the corners. Secure and trim the threads.

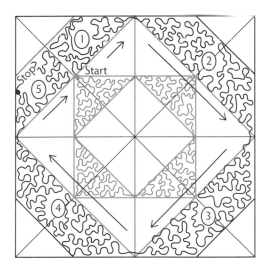

Stipple frame.

Outlining Options

Combining Elements for Fantastic Designs

Half-Corner Frame and Solid Diamond Filler

1. Identify the outer diamond and the inner square (red). Mark the midpoint of the diagonal line on each outer corner (blue). Use the midpoints to draw a line parallel to each side of the outer square to form the frame's outer edge (blue). Mark and connect the midpoints of the inner square's sides to form the filler's outer edge (green). Shade in the sections to be stitched, if desired.

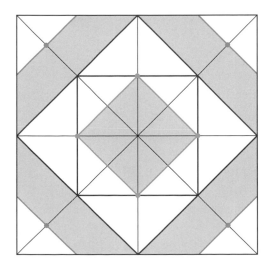

Mark reference lines.

2. If you're not outline stitching the filler, skip to step 3. If you're adding outline stitching, start at one of the inner square's midpoints and outline stitch the filler's outer edge. Leave the needle down at the stopping point.

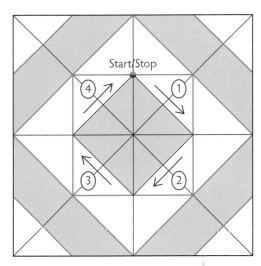

Outline stitch filler.

3. Start at one of the inner square's midpoints (or at the point where you stopped outline stitching) and stipple the inside of the filler. Exit the design at the opposite corner. Secure and trim the threads.

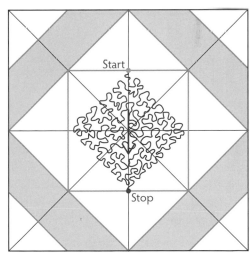

Stipple filler.

4. If you're not outline stitching the frame, skip to step 7. If you're adding outline stitching, start at one corner of the outer diamond and outline stitch the frame's inner edge. Move inside the frame and stipple up to the outer edge of the design.

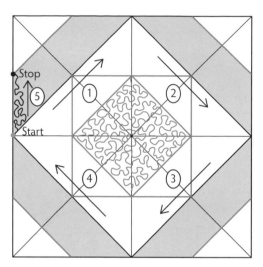

Outline stitch frame.

5. Outline stitch one section of the frame's outer diagonal edge. Move back inside the frame and fill it with stippling, moving to the next section by stitching over the corner.

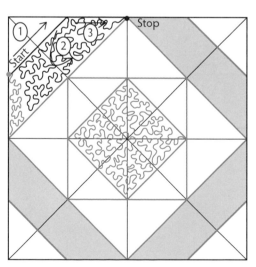

Outline stitch and then stipple first area of frame.

6. Continue around the frame, outline stitching each diagonal edge and then filling in the section with stippling. Secure and trim the threads.

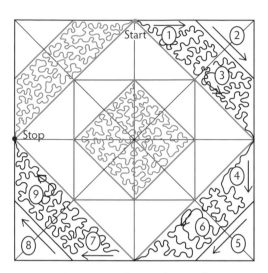

Continue outline stitching and stippling remaining areas of frame.

7. If you're not outline stitching the frame, start stitching at one corner of the outer diamond and fill in the frame design with stippling, moving from one section to another by stitching over the corners. Secure and trim the threads.

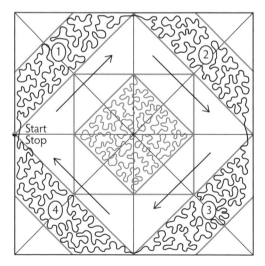

Stipple frame.

Combining Elements for Fantastic Designs

Outlining Options

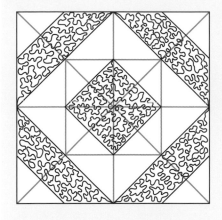  

Combining Elements for Fantastic Designs

Half-Corners Frame and Open Diamond Filler

2. If you're not outline stitching the filler, skip to step 3. If you're adding outline stitching, start at one of the filler's side midpoints and outline stitch the filler's inner and outer edges. Leave the needle down at the stopping point.

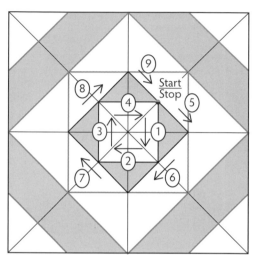

Outline stitch filler.

1. Identify the outer diamond and the inner square (red). Mark the midpoint of the diagonal line on each outer corner (blue). Use the midpoints to draw a line parallel to each side of the outer diamond to form the frame's outer edge (blue). Mark and connect the midpoints of the inner square's sides to form the filler's outer edge (green). Mark and connect the midpoints of the filler's outer edge to form the filler's inner edge (orange). Shade in the sections to be stitched, if desired.

3. Start at one of the filler's side midpoints (or at the point where you stopped outline stitching) and stipple each filler section, moving from one section to another by stitching over the corners. Secure and trim the threads.

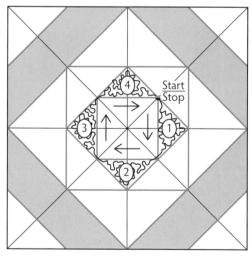

Stipple filler.

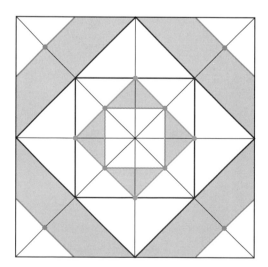

Mark reference lines.

Combining Elements for Fantastic Designs

4. If you're not outline stitching the frame, skip to step 7. If you're adding outline stitching, start at one corner of the outer diamond and outline stitch the frame's inner edge. Move inside the frame and stipple up to the outer edge of the design.

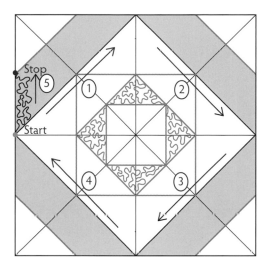

Outline stitch frame.

5. Outline stitch one section of the frame's outer diagonal edge. Move back inside the frame and fill it with stippling, moving to the next section by stitching over the corner.

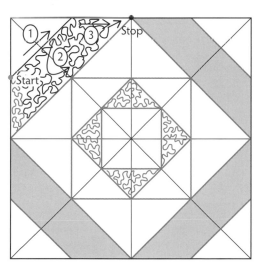

Outline stitch and then stipple first area of frame.

6. Continue around the frame, outline stitching each diagonal edge and then filling in the section with stippling. Secure and trim the threads.

Continue outline stitching and stippling remaining areas of frame.

7. If you're not outline stitching, start at one corner of the outer diamond and fill in the frame design with stippling, moving from one section to another by stitching over the corners. Secure and trim the threads.

Stipple frame.

Combining Elements for Fantastic Designs

Outlining Options

Combining Elements for Fantastic Designs

Inside Border Frame

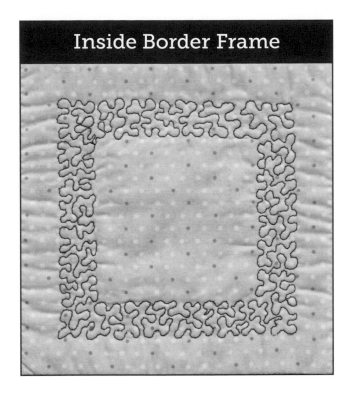

1. Identify the outer diamond and the inner square (red). Mark the midpoints of the diagonal line on each outer corner (blue). Connect the midpoints to form the frame's outer edge (blue). Shade in the sections to be stitched, if desired.

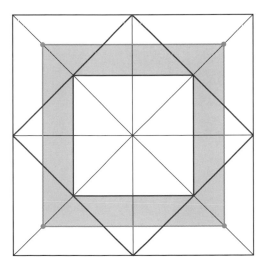

Mark reference lines.

2. If you're not outline stitching the frame, skip to step 3. If you're adding outline stitching, start at one of the inner square's corners and outline stitch the frame's inner edge. Move inside the frame and stipple up to the outer edge of the design (5). Outline stitch the frame's outer edge. Leave the needle down at the stopping point.

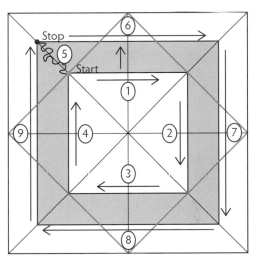

Outline stitch frame.

3. Start at one corner of the inner square (or at the point where you stopped outline stitching) and fill in the frame design with stippling. Secure and trim the threads.

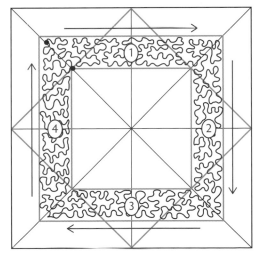

Stipple frame.

Outlining Options

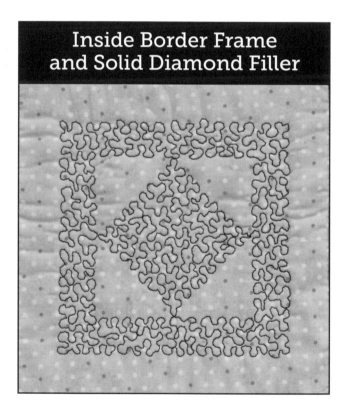

Inside Border Frame and Solid Diamond Filler

1. Identify the outer diamond and the inner square (red). Mark the midpoint of the diagonal line on each outer corner (blue). Connect the midpoints to form the frame's outer edge (blue). Mark and connect the midpoints of the inner square's sides to form the filler's outer edge (green). Shade in the sections to be stitched, if desired.

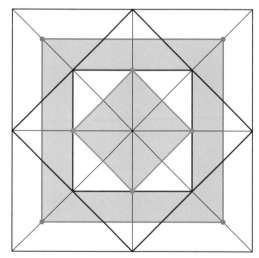

Mark reference lines.

Combining Elements for Fantastic Designs

2. If you're not outline stitching the filler, skip to step 3. If you're adding outline stitching, start at one of the filler's corner points and outline stitch the outer edge. Leave the needle down at the stopping point.

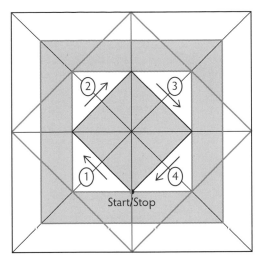

Outline stitch filler.

3. Start at one of the filler's corner points (or at the point where you stopped outline stitching) and stipple the inside of the design. Exit the filler at the opposite corner where it touches the frame. Leave the needle down at the stopping point.

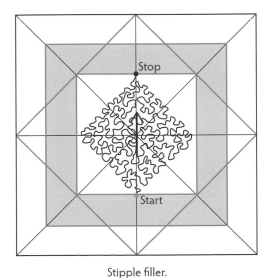

Stipple filler.

4. If you're not outline stitching the frame, skip to step 5. If you're adding outline stitching, continue stitching and outline stitch the frame's inner edge. Move inside the frame and stipple up to the outer edge of the design (5). Outline stitch the frame's outer edge. Leave the needle down at the stopping point.

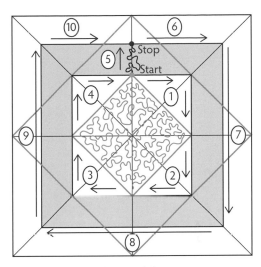

Outline stitch frame.

5. Continue stitching and fill in the frame design with stippling. Secure and trim the threads.

Stipple frame.

Outlining Options

Combining Elements for Fantastic Designs

Inside Border Frame and Open Diamond Filler

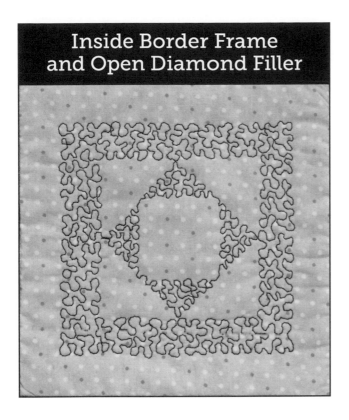

1. Identify the outer diamond and the inner square (red). Mark the midpoint of the diagonal line on each outer corner (blue). Connect the midpoints to create the frame's outer edge (blue). Mark and connect the midpoints of the inner square's sides to form the filler's outer edge (green). Mark and connect the midpoints of the filler's outer edge to form the filler's inner edge (orange). Shade in the sections to be stitched, if desired.

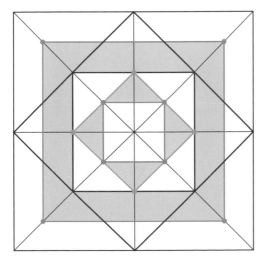

Mark reference lines.

2. If you're not outline stitching the filler, skip to step 3. If you're adding outline stitching, start at one of the filler's side midpoints and outline stitch the filler's inner and outer edges. Leave the needle down at the stopping point.

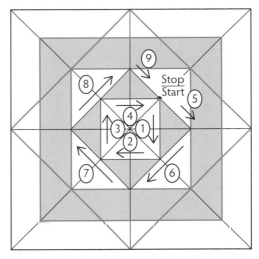

Outline stitch filler.

3. Start at one of the filler's side midpoints (or at the point where you stopped outline stitching) and stipple the inside of each filler section, moving from one section to another by stitching over the corners. Exit the last section where it touches the frame. Leave the needle down at the stopping point.

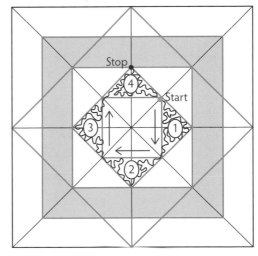

Stipple filler.

4. If you're not outline stitching the frame, skip to step 5. If you're adding outline stitching, continue stitching and outline stitch the frame's inner edge. Move inside the frame and stipple up to the outer edge of the design (5). Outline stitch the frame's outer edge. Leave the needle down at the stopping point.

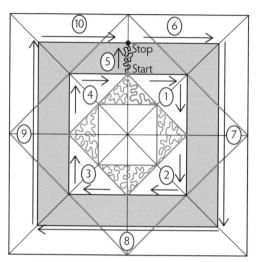

Outline stitch frame.

5. Continue stitching and fill in the frame design with stippling. Secure and trim the threads.

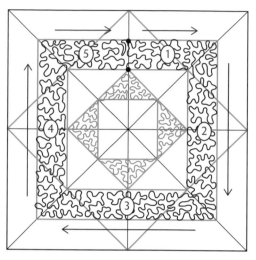

Stipple frame.

Outlining Options

Combining Elements for Fantastic Designs

Inside Border Frame and Solid Square Filler

2. If you're not outline stitching the filler, skip to step 3. If you're adding outline stitching, start at one of the filler's corners and outline stitch the filler's outer edge. Leave the needle down at the stopping point.

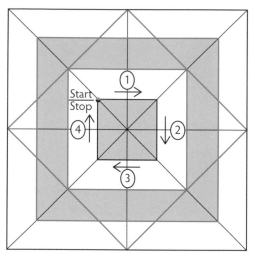

Outline stitch filler.

1. Identify the outer diamond and the inner square (red). Mark the midpoint of the diagonal line in each outer corner (blue). Connect the midpoints to form the frame's outer edge (blue). Mark and connect the midpoints of the inner square's diagonal lines to form the filler's outer edge (green). Shade in the sections to be stitched, if desired.

3. Start at one of the filler's corners (or at the point where you stopped outline stitching) and stipple the inside of the design. Exit the filler at the opposite corner. Secure and trim the threads.

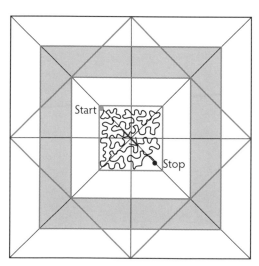

Stipple filler.

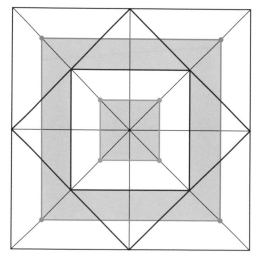

Mark reference lines.

4. If you're not outline stitching the frame, skip to step 5. If you're adding outline stitching, start at one of the inner square's corners and outline stitch the frame's inner edge. Move inside the frame and stipple up to the outer edge of the design (5). Outline stitch the frame's outer edge. Leave the needle down at the stopping point.

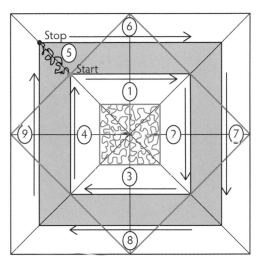

Outline stitch frame.

5. Start at one of the inner square's corners (or at the point where you stopped outline stitching) and fill in the frame design with stippling. Secure and trim the threads.

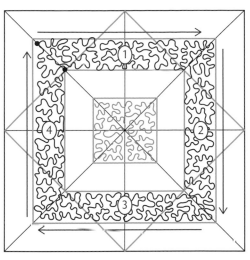

Stipple frame.

Outlining Options

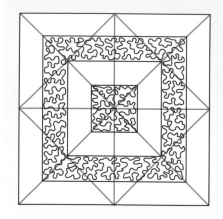  

  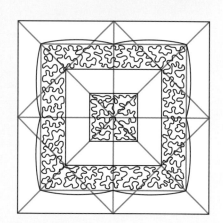

Combining Elements for Fantastic Designs

Inside Border Frame and Corner Squares Variation

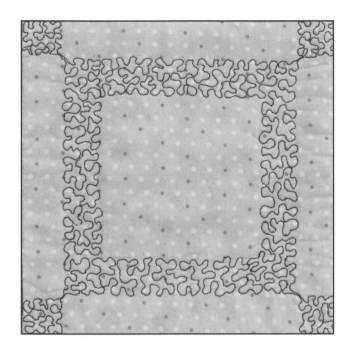

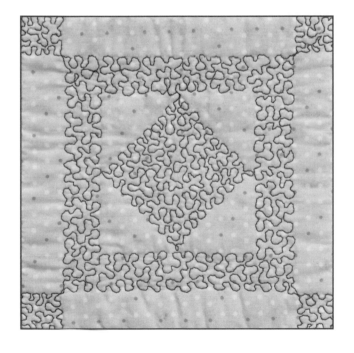

These steps are for stitching the filled corner squares only and can be used with any of the previous instructions for the inside border frame and filler designs.

1. Referring to step 1 of the instructions for the selected inside border frame and filler, mark the block(s). Extend the lines that form the outer frame to the outer edges of the quilt block (red). Stitch the filler design (if applicable).

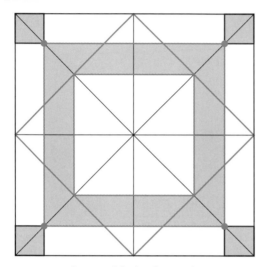

Mark corner block reference lines.

2. If you're not adding outline stitching to the frame, skip to step 3. If you're adding outline stitching, follow the instructions for the selected frame, and stop when you get to the instructions for outline stitching the outer edges of the frame.

   Stitch the first outer edge of the frame up to the first corner square (1). Exit the frame at the corner square and outline stitch one of the square's sides (2). Fill the square with stippling, exiting at the opposite side (3). Outline stitch the square's other side (4). Outline stitch the next outer edge of the frame (5).

Repeat the corner square stitching for the remaining corners and frame edge (6). Continue stitching and fill the frame with stippling (7). Secure and trim the threads.

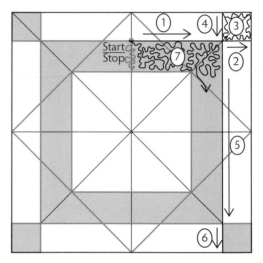

Outline stitch frame and corner blocks.

3. If you're not adding outline stitching, follow the instructions for the selected frame, with or without a filler and stipple each section of the design. As you come to an outer corner of the frame, exit the frame at the corner square and enter the corner block. Fill it with stippling and then return to the frame at the entry point.

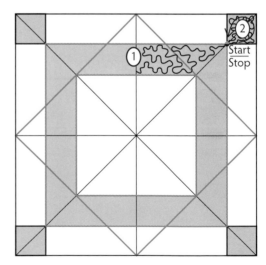

Stipple frame and corner block.

4. Continue around the rest of the frame in the same manner. Secure and trim the threads.

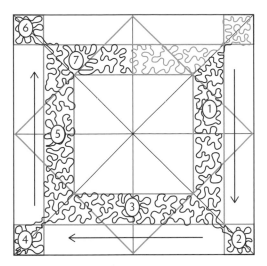

Stipple remainder of
frame and corner blocks.

Outlining Options

The frames and fillers work in any style or shape block, whether it's pieced or plain, so "quilt as desired" is no longer a problem but an exciting decision. The hardest part can be choosing which design to use, but the blocks themselves can help narrow down the choices.

Consider the size of the block. The block size determines the amount of quilting space available, which in turn helps determine the design details that are needed. The goal is to achieve a balance between the two. As a general rule, I feel there should be equal amounts of quilting and open space not only in the blocks, but in the overall quilt as well.

Notice how adding an inner filler section of quilting makes a large block look more balanced.

Large (12") quilt block underquilted

A filler design gives this small (4") block just the right amount of quilting in relation to open space.

Evaluate the number of seams. Heavily pieced blocks can make quilting more difficult. The needle tends to get stuck in the seam allowances and a large jump stitch can form when you stitch over them. I recommend using a less complicated frame-and-filler design and eliminating any outline stitching.

Determine if the print will hide the quilting. The busier the fabric, the less prominence your quilting will have. Personally, I don't add a lot of stitch detail when a fabric won't show the design. I prefer to quilt something simple so the area still has texture.

AUDITIONING THE DESIGN

I like to have an idea of how a design will look in a block before I commit to stitching it. There are a couple of easy ways to audition designs. One option is to make a photocopy of the actual quilt block from the quilt or the pattern and draw the frame and/or filler on it. The other option is to actually draw the frame on the quilt block with your fabric-marking pens. By drawing the design on the block, you're able to see if the design fills the space evenly and has a natural flow. Plus, it's a lot easier to fine-tune your design at this point than to have to take out actual stitches later on down the road!

Quilt block marked with Star frame and Solid Diamond filler design

MAPPING THE DESIGN

Before you actually stitch the designs on your quilt top, draw them on paper first. Use the drawn design to map out your quilting path with numbers. This allows you to become more comfortable with where you'll be heading and stopping. This is especially helpful to me when I'm adding outline stitching. I'm a more visual person, so I benefit from having something to look at while I'm quilting.

Follow these steps to help you map out your design before quilting.

1. Select the design.
2. Draw the grid on paper as outlined in the design instructions, including the starting and stopping points.
3. Shade in the frame and filler or fill them with a stippling design (this is a great way to practice).
4. Draw in the outline stitching, if applicable.
5. Add any numbers or reference points to make the quilting easier.

Don't Forget to Warm Up

Before you start free-motion quilting, it's a good idea to review the basics, practice drawing the stipple designs, and then do a few minutes of actual stippling. For most of us, these few minutes are necessary to get back into the flow of things.

"Flowers and Baskets"

Four Corners frame

"Birds All Around"

Inside Border frame with Solid Square filler

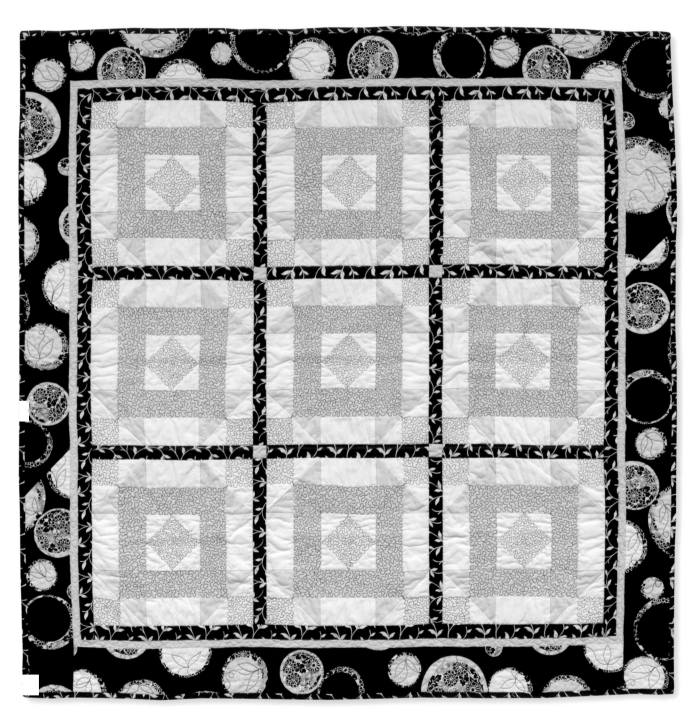

"Churn Dash"

*Inside Border frame with
corner blocks variation
and Solid Diamond filler*

*Quilting detail
on back of quilt*

"Pinwheel"

**Double Diamond frame with
curved outline stitching**

"Double Wedding Ring"

Star frame and Solid Diamond filler
with curved outline stitching

"Home Among the Vines,"
pattern by Alma Allen and
Barb Adams of Blackbird Designs

Star frame with free-form filler design and
straight and curved outline stitching

Gallery

*"Charmed Star," pattern
by Kathy Love of Quilt Patterns*

*Four Triangles frame and Solid Diamond
filler with curved outline stitching*

"Log Cabin Quilt"

*Four Triangles frame and Solid Diamond
filler with curved outline stitching*

Quilting detail on back of quilt

"Nine Patch Posey"

*Half-Corners frame and Solid Square
filler with straight outline stitching (top).
Inner Border frame with straight
and curved outline stitching (bottom).*

Sampler quilt showcasing a variety of quilting designs

Eva Larkin started quilting in 1999 while living in Australia, but it wasn't until she moved back to the United States in 2002 that she took her first class on free-motion quilting. She wasn't a natural at it and struggled, like most people, with the basics (thread tension, stitch length, and design consistency). For the next several years she bought whatever books she could find on the subject, took additional classes, and "practiced" in order to improve her stippling skills. In 2003 she started working in a quilt store and slowly developed a small quilting business. During this time as a professional quilter she finally developed an understanding of the basics of free-motion quilting and began teaching classes to pass these fundamentals on to others. Her goal was to make the learning process for her students less frustrating than it had been for herself. She wanted to give them information they could understand and exercises they could actually practice that would help them see an improvement in their free-motion skills. She also began to develop quilting designs that could be successfully executed on a domestic sewing machine, which she used in her business instead of a long-arm quilting machine. Her ambition was to develop designs that the everyday quilter, like herself, could consistently quilt without spending a lot of time practicing. These design ideas are the foundation for her books. Her favorite phrase is "You can do it!" and she uses it often when teaching classes or sharing ideas with other quilters on free-motion quilting designs. She truly believes that anyone who wants to can free-motion quilt and achieve good results!

Visit Eva at www.evalarkin.com.